I0018912

The Simplified Guide to Wix Website Design for Beginners and Pros:

Step-by-Step to Success

Mega Jammy

Mega Jammy

Mega Jammy

Table of Contents

Mega Jammy

Mega Jammy

Mega Jammy

Introduction: Your Website, Your Power, Your Future

When I built my first website, I was overwhelmed. I had a vision in my head—a sleek, professional, and engaging site that would represent my business and passion. But I didn't have a clue where to begin. Like many, I thought building a website required years of coding experience, expensive developers, and a deep understanding of technology. The fear of doing it wrong kept me frozen, staring at a blank screen, wondering if I'd ever bring my ideas to life.

Does this sound familiar? If you've ever dreamed of creating a stunning website but felt uncertain, you're not alone. The good news? That fear, that hesitation, ends today.

This book is your guide, your mentor, and your toolkit. Whether you're a complete beginner or someone who has dabbled in website design before, I'm here to tell you one thing: **You can do this.** And Wix is the perfect platform to make it happen.

Mega Jammy

The Power of Your Online Presence

Think about the last time you wanted to learn more about a business, a product, or a person. What did you do? You probably searched for them online. And what happens when there's no website? A business without a website is like a store without a sign—people don't know it exists. Worse, if your website looks outdated, unprofessional, or confusing, it can drive potential customers away faster than you can say "bounce rate."

But here's the exciting part: Your website isn't just a place to display information. It's a digital extension of your brand, voice, and story. It's how you connect with customers, readers, or fans. It's your chance to **stand out** in a noisy world and create something uniquely yours.

Wix makes this process easier than ever. Its platform empowers you to design without limits, without needing to learn complex coding, and without breaking the bank on developers. But simply having access to Wix isn't enough—you need a **strategy** to create a site that works. That's exactly what this book is here to teach you.

The Moment That Changed Everything

A few years ago, I met a young entrepreneur named Sarah. She had a small candle-making business, creating hand-poured, eco-friendly candles from her home. She poured her heart and soul into her craft, but no one beyond her immediate circle knew she existed.

"I tried building a website once," she admitted over coffee, "but it looked so bad that I gave up. I thought maybe I just wasn't meant to have one."

Sarah's problem wasn't a lack of talent—it was a lack of guidance. So, we sat down and started from scratch. Using Wix, we crafted a beautiful, user-friendly online store that showcased her products in the best light possible. Within weeks of launching, she had her first big sale. A few months later, her website generated more revenue than ever imagined. Today, she's running a thriving online business because she took that one step.

Sarah's story proves anyone can build a powerful website with the right tools and direction. And if she could do it, so can you.

The Biggest Myths About Building a Website

Before we dive into the step-by-step process of designing your Wix site, let's clear up some of the biggest misconceptions holding you back:

Myth #1: You Need to Know How to Code. Not true! Wix's drag-and-drop builder allows you to create stunning sites without writing a single line of code. You don't need to be a tech expert—just someone with a vision and a willingness to learn.

Myth #2: Websites Take Months to Build. Many assume they'll have to spend endless hours perfecting their site before it can go live. But with Wix's intuitive tools, you can create a functional, professional-looking site in just a few days (or even hours!).

Myth #3: If You Build It, They Will Come. Having a website is one thing—getting people to visit it is another. That's why this book doesn't just teach you how to design a website; it also covers **SEO, marketing, and growth strategies** to ensure your site gets the attention it deserves.

Myth #4: It's Too Late to Start. Whether launching a business, building a personal brand, or creating a passion project, the best time to start is **now**. The internet is always evolving, and there's room for **you** to carve out your own space.

What You'll Learn in This Book

Throughout these pages, you'll discover **everything you need** to build a successful website on Wix from start to finish. We'll cover:

- **Choosing the right design** for your brand

- **Optimizing your site for search engines (SEO)** to increase visibility

- **Creating a user-friendly experience** that keeps visitors engaged

- **Setting up an online store** that sells

- **Avoiding common mistakes** that make websites look unprofessional

- **Using Wix's latest tools and updates** to stay ahead of the competition

- **Scaling your site over time** to grow your audience and business

By the time you finish this book, you won't just have a website—you'll have a **powerful online presence** that sets you apart.

Your Journey Starts Now

If you've made it this far, you're serious about building something great. You're ready to take control of your online success and create a website that works for you, not against you. And you won't be doing it alone—I'll be with you every step of the way, guiding you through the process with practical, easy-to-follow advice.

So, take a deep breath. Picture your dream website. Imagine how it will feel when you finally launch it and see visitors engaging with your content, buying your products, or reaching out to connect with you.

That future is within reach. Let's build it together.

Chapter 1: Why Wix? The Best Website Builder for All Levels

Imagine waking up one day with a brilliant idea—an idea that has the potential to transform your life or business. Maybe it's an online store, a blog, a portfolio to showcase your skills, or a personal project you want the world to see. You're excited and ready to take action, but there's one problem: you don't know how to build a website. The thought of coding sounds intimidating, and hiring a professional seems expensive. This is where Wix comes in—the website builder that has revolutionized how people create and manage websites, regardless of their skill level.

Building a website used to be a daunting task. It required extensive technical knowledge, coding experience, and significant time and money. But today, thanks to platforms like Wix, anyone can design and publish a professional-looking website without writing a single line of code. Whether you're a complete beginner or an experienced designer looking for a fast and efficient solution, Wix offers the tools and flexibility to bring your vision to life.

With so many website-building platforms available today, why should you choose Wix? The answer is simple: Wix combines ease of use with powerful features, making it one of the most user-friendly and versatile website builders.

1. User-Friendly Drag-and-Drop Interface

Wix is designed for people who want complete control over their website's look and feel without dealing with complicated coding. Its intuitive drag-and-drop editor allows you to move elements around freely, customize layouts, and experiment with designs effortlessly. Whether you want to add text, images, videos, or forms, it's all as simple as dragging and dropping.

2. Professionally Designed Templates

Starting from scratch can feel overwhelming, but Wix provides over 800 designer-made templates that cater to various industries. Whether you're a photographer, entrepreneur, blogger, or restaurateur, there's a template designed to suit your needs. Each template is fully customizable, allowing you to tweak colors, fonts, and layouts to match your brand's identity.

3. Powerful SEO and Marketing Tools

A website isn't just about looking good—it must be discovered. Wix includes built-in SEO (Search Engine Optimization) tools to help your site rank on Google. With customizable meta tags, alt text for images, and automatic mobile optimization, your website stands a better chance of reaching the right audience. Additionally, Wix offers marketing integrations like email campaigns, social media connectivity, and analytics to track visitor behavior.

4. Wix ADI vs. Wix Editor: Choose Your Path

Wix offers two main ways to build a website:

- **Wix ADI (Artificial Design Intelligence):** This service is perfect for beginners who want a website up and running quickly. Just answer a few questions, and Wix ADI automatically generates a fully functional website tailored to your needs.

- **Wix Editor:** This tool offers complete creative freedom. You can start with a blank canvas or a template and customize every detail to create a unique, professional site.

5. Scalability and Business Growth

Wix isn't just for personal websites. It provides tools for e-commerce, online bookings, memberships, and subscriptions, making it an ideal choice for business owners looking to grow. Whether you need a simple portfolio or a full-fledged online store, Wix scales with your needs.

What This Book Will Teach You (Beginners to Advanced Users)

This book is designed to take you from a complete beginner to a confident Wix user capable of easily designing and managing a professional website. Here's what you can expect to learn:

For Beginners:

- How to sign up for Wix and choose the best pricing plan.

- Navigating the Wix dashboard and understanding the basic tools.

- Selecting and customizing a template to fit your needs.

- Adding essential elements like text, images, and buttons.

- Connecting your website to a domain and publishing it.

For Intermediate Users:

- Advanced customization with Wix Editor.

- Implementing SEO strategies to improve search rankings.

- Integrating third-party apps for additional functionality.

- Adding interactive elements such as contact forms, booking systems, and blogs.

- Mobile optimization to ensure a seamless experience for all devices.

For Advanced Users:

- Mastering Wix Code (Velo) for custom web applications.

- Automating workflows with Wix's built-in tools.

- Creating dynamic pages and databases for scalable websites.

- Managing e-commerce stores, setting up payments, and tracking sales.

- Troubleshooting and optimizing website performance.

No matter your level of experience, this book will provide step-by-step guidance for efficiently building and maintaining a stunning Wix website.

How to Get the Most Out of This Guide

To make the most of this book, follow these practical tips:

1. Follow Along Step-by-Step

Applying what you learn in real-time rather than just reading through the chapters. Open Wix in your browser and practice each step as you progress.

2. Experiment and Customize

The best way to learn Wix is by experimenting. Try different layouts, color schemes, and features to see what works best.

3. Take Notes and Bookmark Key Sections

If you encounter a feature or tip, you want to revisit later, make notes or bookmark the section for quick access.

Mega Jammy

4. Use Wix's Support and Community

Wix has an active help center and a community forum where you can ask questions and get additional support. If you ever get stuck, don't hesitate to seek help.

5. Stay Updated with New Features

Wix frequently updates its platform with new tools and functionalities. Keep an eye on updates to ensure you're using the latest features.

By following this guide, you'll learn how to create a Wix website and optimize, manage, and grow it effectively. Whether you're looking to build a personal blog, an online store, or a portfolio, this book will equip you with the knowledge and confidence to make your vision a reality.

Let's get started!

Chapter 2: Understanding Wix and Choosing the Right Plan

What is Wix? A Brief Overview

Wix is a leading website builder that empowers users to create stunning, professional-looking websites without coding expertise. Whether you're a small business owner, freelancer, blogger, or e-commerce entrepreneur, Wix offers a versatile platform that accommodates various needs. Launched in 2006, Wix has become one of the most user-friendly and feature-rich website builders. Its drag-and-drop interface, extensive template collection, and AI-powered design tools make it an excellent choice for beginners and experienced users.

Unlike traditional web development methods that require knowledge of HTML, CSS, and JavaScript, Wix simplifies the process by allowing users to design and launch a website through an intuitive interface. With its vast app market, built-in SEO tools, and mobile optimization features, Wix ensures your website is functional, attractive, and easy to manage.

Comparing Wix vs. Other Website Builders (WordPress, Squarespace, Shopify)

Choosing the right website builder is crucial, as each platform has strengths and weaknesses. Let's compare Wix to some of the most popular alternatives.

Wix vs. WordPress

WordPress is an open-source content management system (CMS) that offers immense customization and flexibility. While WordPress is ideal for complex websites, it requires technical expertise, domain hosting, and ongoing maintenance. Wix, on the other hand, provides an all-in-one platform with built-in hosting, design tools, and customer support. If you're looking for a user-friendly experience with minimal setup, Wix is the better option.

Wix vs. Squarespace

Squarespace is another popular website builder known for its sleek and modern designs. While both platforms offer beautiful templates and easy-to-use interfaces, Wix provides more design freedom and a larger app marketplace. Wix's AI-powered Wix ADI and Editor X cater to different user levels, whereas Squarespace follows a more structured approach to design.

Wix vs. Shopify

Shopify is primarily an e-commerce platform, making it the go-to choice for businesses selling products online. However, Wix also offers powerful e-commerce features, including customizable online stores, multiple payment options, and marketing tools. For small businesses and individuals looking for a multipurpose website with integrated e-commerce, Wix provides a cost-effective alternative.

Choosing the Best Wix Plan for Your Needs (Free vs. Premium)

Wix offers multiple pricing tiers to cater to different user needs. Here's a breakdown of the options available:

Free Plan

The free plan allows you to create a website without cost, but it has limitations. Your site will have Wix-branded domain names (e.g., username.wixsite.com/sitename), and Wix ads will be displayed on your pages. While this plan is great for

16

experimenting, businesses and serious website owners should consider upgrading to a premium plan for better customization and branding.

Premium Plans

Wix provides various premium plans with enhanced features, including custom domains, additional storage, and access to advanced marketing tools. The main premium plans include:

- **Combo Plan**—This plan is best for personal use. It removes Wix ads, provides a free domain for a year, and includes 3GB storage.

- **Unlimited Plan**—Ideal for freelancers and entrepreneurs, this plan offers unlimited bandwidth, 10GB storage, and additional marketing features.

- **Pro Plan**—Designed for businesses that require advanced branding and analytics, this plan includes a professional logo and social media logo files.

- **VIP Plan** – The highest-tier plan with priority customer support, increased storage, and marketing tools.

17

- **Business & E-commerce Plans**—These plans are specifically for online stores and allow you to accept online payments, offer advanced e-commerce tools, and manage your store efficiently.

How to Save Money on Wix Plans

If you're looking to reduce costs while using Wix, consider the following tips:

- **Utilize Discounts & Promotions**—Wix frequently offers discounts on annual plans. Look for seasonal promotions to save on subscription fees.

- **Choose an Annual Plan** – Paying for a full year upfront is often more cost-effective than monthly billing.

- **Use the Free Plan for Testing**—Before committing to a paid plan, explore Wix's features using the free version. This will allow you to determine whether the platform meets your needs.

- **Only Upgrade When Necessary** – If you start with a basic premium plan, you can

18

upgrade as your website grows. Avoid overspending on features you don't need initially.

- **Take Advantage of Free Apps** – Wix has an extensive marketplace with free and premium apps. Look for free alternatives to enhance your site's functionality.

By selecting the right Wix plan and utilizing cost-saving strategies, you can build a high-quality website without exceeding your budget. Wix provides an excellent balance between affordability and powerful website-building tools, making it a top choice for individuals and businesses.

Chapter 3: Setting Up Your Wix Account
How to Sign Up and Choose a Website Template

Creating your Wix account is the first step toward building your professional or personal website. Wix makes this process simple and user-friendly. To get started, visit Wix.com and click on the **Sign Up** button. You can register using your email, Google account, or Facebook account.

Once logged in, Wix will ask a few questions to understand the purpose of your website. This helps recommend the most suitable design options. You'll then have the option to create your site using **Wix ADI (Artificial Design Intelligence)** or manually select a **template** and customize it using the Wix Editor.

Wix offers hundreds of professionally designed templates across industries such as business, portfolio, e-commerce, blogs, etc. When choosing a template, consider:

- **Your Industry** – Pick a template that aligns with your niche to minimize design adjustments.

20

- **Functionality** – Ensure the template supports your needed features, such as e-commerce tools, booking systems, or blogs.

- **Aesthetic Appeal** – Select a layout that matches your brand identity and preferred color scheme.

It's essential to note that once you choose a template, you won't be able to switch to a different one later without redesigning the site from scratch.

Understanding the Wix Dashboard and Tools

After selecting a template, you'll land on the **Wix Dashboard**, which serves as your website's control panel. Here, you can manage your site's settings, domain, SEO, and more.

Key sections of the Wix Dashboard include:

- **Site Overview** – Provides analytics, traffic insights, and performance data.

- **Site Actions** – You can publish, preview, duplicate, or delete your site.

- **Settings** – This lets you configure domains, business information, roles and permissions, and marketing tools.

- **App Market**—This allows you to integrate third-party apps for additional functionality, such as chatbots, social media feeds, and appointment bookings.

- **Wix Editor & Wix ADI** – Access these tools to customize your website design and content.

Familiarizing yourself with these tools will ensure you efficiently manage your website and enhance its features as needed.

Wix ADI vs. Wix Editor: Which One Should You Use?

Wix offers two website-building methods: **Wix ADI** and **Wix Editor**. Understanding the differences will help you determine the best option for your needs.

Wix ADI (Artificial Design Intelligence)

Wix ADI is an automated tool that creates a website for you based on the answers you provide during setup. It is ideal for beginners who want a website quickly without diving into design and customization.

Mega Jammy

Pros of Wix ADI:

- Fully automated site creation.

- No design skills required.

- Mobile-friendly by default.

- Saves time with pre-built layouts and content suggestions.

Cons of Wix ADI:

- Limited customization options.

- Less flexibility compared to Wix Editor.

- Might not fully capture your vision if you have a specific design.

Wix Editor

Wix Editor is a drag-and-drop design tool that gives users full control over their website's layout, fonts, colors, images, and functionality. It is perfect for users who want creative freedom and advanced design features.

Pros of Wix Editor:

- Complete control over design and layout.

- Access to advanced design tools.

- Ability to add custom code and third-party integrations.

- Ideal for unique, personalized websites.

Cons of Wix Editor:

- Requires time to learn and master.

- Can be overwhelming for beginners.

Which One Should You Choose?

- If you **want a simple, hands-off approach**, Wix ADI is your best bet.

- If you **prefer full creative control**, go with Wix Editor.

Essential First Steps Before You Start Designing

Before jumping into the website design process, a few key steps will set you up for success.

1. Define Your Website Goals

Clarify the purpose of your website. Are you building a portfolio, selling products, offering services, or running a blog? Defining your goals helps you structure the content and select the right features.

2. Gather Your Branding Materials

To maintain consistency, prepare branding elements such as:

- **Logo** (Use Wix's Logo Maker if you don't have one)

- **Color scheme** (Ensure it aligns with your brand identity)

- **Fonts** (Pick readable and professional fonts)

- **Images & Videos** (Use high-quality visuals for better engagement)

3. Plan Your Website Structure

A well-structured website improves user experience. Sketch a sitemap outlining the key pages you need, such as:

- Home

- About Us

- Services/Products

- Blog

- Contact

4. Secure a Custom Domain

While Wix provides a free domain (e.g., username.wixsite.com), a custom domain (e.g., yourbusiness.com) adds professionalism. You can purchase one through Wix or connect an existing domain.

5. Optimize for Mobile Users

Wix sites are mobile-responsive, but you should preview your design on mobile devices to ensure optimal display and functionality.

By following these steps, you'll be well-prepared to start designing a high-quality, professional website using Wix. In the next chapters, we'll dive deeper into customization techniques, SEO optimization, and advanced features to take your site to the next level.

Chapter 4: Mastering the Wix Editor (Step-by-Step with Screenshots)

Navigating the Wix Interface

When you first enter the **Wix Editor**, it may seem overwhelming, but it's designed to be user-friendly. The interface is divided into three main sections:

1. **Left Sidebar** – You can add elements like text, images, buttons, and more.

2. **Top Toolbar** – Allows quick access to undo/redo, preview, and site settings.

3. **Canvas (Main Editing Area)** – This is where you design your website in real-time.

To start, take a few minutes to hover over each icon and explore its functions. Wix provides tooltips that help explain each feature's function.

How to Use Wix Drag-and-Drop Features

One of the biggest advantages of Wix is its **drag-and-drop functionality**. Unlike traditional web design that requires coding, Wix lets you drag elements from the sidebar and drop them anywhere on your page.

Mega Jammy

Step-by-Step Guide:

1. Click the **"Add" (+) button** on the left sidebar.

2. Select an element you want to add (e.g., text, image, button).

3. Drag it onto your canvas.

4. Resize and reposition it as needed.

Example:

Imagine you're designing a bakery homepage. You can drag a beautiful high-resolution image of cupcakes, add a heading like "Freshly Baked Every Morning," and position it centrally on the page.

Adding and Customizing Text, Images, and Videos

Text, images, and videos are the heart of your website. Here's how you can easily add and customize them in Wix.

Adding Text:

1. Click the **"Add" button** on the left sidebar.

2. Select **Text** and choose a heading, paragraph, or a custom font style.

3. Drag it onto your canvas and type your content.

4. Use the **Text Settings** to adjust font, color, spacing, and alignment.

Example:

A photography portfolio site might use bold typography like "Capturing Life's Best Moments" with a clean, modern font.

Adding Images:

1. Click on **"Add"** > **"Image"** from the left sidebar.

2. Choose from Wix's free image library or upload your own.

3. Drag the image into place and resize as needed.

Example:

An online store can display high-quality product images with hover effects to showcase different angles.

Adding Videos:

1. Click on **"Add"** > **"Video"**.

2. Upload your video or embed it from YouTube/Vimeo.

3. Adjust the size, autoplay, and loop settings.

Working with Backgrounds and Colors to Enhance Your Brand

The right colors and backgrounds make your website visually appealing and reinforce your brand identity.

Changing Backgrounds:

1. Click on **"Background"** in the left sidebar.

2. Choose a solid color, gradient, image, or video background.

3. Adjust transparency and effects for a unique look.

Example:

A travel blog can use a high-resolution video background of a beach to create a lively, immersive experience.

Choosing a Color Palette:

- Wix allows you to set a **site-wide color theme**.

- Click on **"Site Design"** > **"Color"** and select a palette that matches your brand.

Mastering the **Wix Editor** is about practice and creativity. Experiment with different features, explore customization options and build a website representing your vision.

Quick Tip:

Use the **Preview** feature frequently to see how your design looks in real time before publishing!

Chapter 5: Building a Strong Website Structure

A well-structured website is like a well-organized store—visitors should find what they need quickly and effortlessly. Without a strong structure, even the most visually stunning site can become confusing, leading to high bounce rates and lost potential customers. Wix provides powerful tools to help you organize your website efficiently. This chapter covers creating and structuring pages, effectively using Wix strips and sections, building easy-to-navigate menus, and customizing headers and footers to improve usability.

Creating and Organizing Pages

Your website's pages are the foundation of your online presence. Whether you're building a blog, portfolio, business site, or online store, each page should serve a purpose and flow logically from one to another.

Steps to Create and Organize Pages in Wix

1. **Access the Pages Panel:** Open the Wix Editor and click on the "Pages & Menu" tab on the left sidebar. This is where you can add, remove, and organize pages.

2. **Add New Pages:** Click "+ Add Page" and choose the type of page you want (blank page, predefined layout, or dynamic page).

3. **Name Your Pages Clearly:** Use clear, SEO-friendly names. For example, instead of naming a page "Stuff," call it "Our Services" or "Product Catalog."

4. **Organize Pages in a Logical Order:** Prioritize the most important pages (Home, About, Contact, Services) at the top of your menu.

5. **Use Subpages to Group Related Content:** Drag and drop pages under a main page to create dropdown menus, keeping navigation clean and intuitive.

6. **Set Page Permissions:** Wix allows you to control who can view certain pages. This is useful for member-only content or premium subscriptions.

Example of a Well-Structured Website Page Layout

- Home

- About Us

- Services

  - ○ Web Design

  - ○ SEO Services

  - ○ Content Marketing

- Blog

- Contact Us

How to Use Wix Strips and Sections Effectively

Wix strips and sections help you structure your content in a visually appealing and user-friendly way. Instead of cramming everything into one block, you can break content into digestible sections that enhance readability.

What Are Wix Strips?

Strips are full-width sections that can hold text, images, videos, and widgets. They allow you to create a structured, professional layout without complex coding.

How to Add and Customize Wix Strips

1. **Open the Wix Editor:** Click the "+" button to add elements.

2. **Select "Strip" from the Elements Menu. You can Choose from various pre-designed strips, such as** testimonials, image galleries, or contact sections.

3. **Customize the Strip:** Change the background (color, image, or video), adjust the height, and add elements such as text, buttons, or forms.

4. **Rearrange Strips for Better Flow:** Drag and drop strips to reposition them for an optimal user experience.

Using Sections for Better Organization

Sections within strips allow you to organize content into easily scannable chunks. For example, you can have a strip for "Our Services" and use sections to highlight individual offerings.

Best Practices for Using Wix Strips and Sections:

- Keep each strip focused on a single topic.

- Use contrasting backgrounds to differentiate sections.

- Add padding and spacing for a clean design.

- Maintain a logical reading flow from top to bottom.

Adding Navigation Menus for Easy Browsing

A user-friendly navigation menu is essential for keeping visitors engaged. If users struggle to find what they need, they'll leave quickly.

Steps to Create and Customize Navigation Menus

1. **Access the Menu Settings:** Click "Menus & Pages" in the left panel.

2. **Choose a Menu Style:** Wix offers horizontal, vertical, and hamburger menus (ideal for mobile sites).

Mega Jammy

3. **Drag and Drop to Organize:** Arrange menu items logically based on importance and user flow.

4. **Create Dropdown Menus:** Nest-related pages under parent pages to reduce clutter.

5. **Highlight Important Pages:** Use buttons or bold colors to highlight key pages like "Sign Up" or "Shop Now."

Example of an Effective Navigation Menu

- Home

- Services

  o Web Development

  o Branding & Identity

- Blog

- Portfolio

- Contact

Pro Tip: Ensure all links are working properly, and keep the menu consistent across all pages.

Understanding Header and Footer Customization

Headers and footers are on every page, making them crucial for navigation and branding.

Customizing the Header

1. **Click on the Header in Wix Editor:** Choose "Customize Header."

2. **Add Your Logo:** A strong brand identity starts with a visible, well-placed logo.

3. **Keep the Navigation Simple:** Avoid overcrowding the header with unnecessary elements.

4. **Use a Sticky Header:** This keeps the menu visible as users scroll.

Customizing the Footer

1. **Click on the Footer Area:** Select "Edit Footer."

2. **Include Essential Information:** Add business contact details, social media links, and a sitemap.

3. **Use Consistent Colors and Fonts:** Ensure the footer aligns with the website's design.

4. **Add a Call to Action:** Encourage users to subscribe, follow, or get in touch.

A well-structured website makes a world of difference in user experience and engagement. By strategically organizing pages, effectively using Wix strips and sections, setting up intuitive navigation menus, and optimizing headers and footers, you ensure a seamless browsing experience. Implement these best practices, and you'll build a beautiful and highly functional website.

Now that your website structure is set up, let's explore content creation and customization in more detail in the next chapter!

Chapter 6: Advanced Design Features & Customization
Using Wix's AI Design Assistant for Faster Website Creation

One of Wix's most powerful tools is its AI-powered design assistant, known as Wix ADI (Artificial Design Intelligence). This feature allows you to create a fully designed website within minutes by answering a few simple questions about your business or project. Unlike traditional website builders that require you to choose templates and manually adjust layouts, Wix ADI does the heavy lifting for you.

How to Use Wix ADI:

1. **Start from Scratch or Convert an Existing Site** – When setting up your website, Wix will offer you two options: using Wix ADI or customizing a template with the classic Wix Editor.

2. **Answer a Few Questions** – The ADI will ask you about the purpose of your website, the type of industry you're in, and any features you want (such as an online store, blog, or portfolio).

40

3. **AI-Powered Customization** – Based on your responses, Wix ADI will generate a professional-looking website with a layout, color scheme, and content suggestions.

4. **Fine-Tune the Details** – While Wix ADI does a great job at creating a functional site, you can still tweak the design, change colors, adjust fonts, and replace images to match your brand identity.

Wix ADI is ideal for those who want a professional-looking site with minimal effort, but if you need more control over design elements, the traditional Wix Editor is the better choice.

Adding Animations and Interactive Elements

Adding animations and interactive elements to your Wix website can make it more engaging and visually appealing. Wix offers built-in animation features that allow you to animate text, images, buttons, and entire sections.

How to Add Animations:

1. **Select an Element** – Click on the text, image, or button you want to animate.

2. **Click on the Animation Icon** – This will open a menu where you can choose different animation styles.

3. **Choose an Animation Effect** – Wix offers various options such as fade-in, slide-in, bounce, and zoom effects.

4. **Adjust Timing and Speed** – Control the duration and delay of the animation to create a smooth effect.

Animations can be a great way to highlight key sections of your website, but they should be used sparingly to avoid slowing down page load times.

Interactive Features You Can Add:

- **Hover Effects** – Make buttons or images change when hovered over.

- **Parallax Scrolling** – Create depth by making background images move at a different speed than foreground elements.

Mega Jammy

- **Click-to-Reveal Content** – Hide certain sections and reveal them when users click a button or link.

- **Custom Popups** – Create popups that appear when users perform specific actions (e.g., visiting a page for the first time).

How to Use Wix's Design Tools Like a Pro (Grids, Layers, and Effects)

To truly master Wix design, you need to understand its advanced tools, including grids, layers, and visual effects.

Using Grids for Precise Layouts

Grids help you structure your content in a visually balanced way. They create alignment guides, ensuring that images, text, and buttons are evenly spaced.

- **How to Enable Grids** – Go to the Wix Editor, click on "Tools" in the top menu, and enable "Gridlines."

- **Align Elements to Grid** – When dragging elements, they will snap to the gridlines for perfect alignment.

- **Use Column-Based Layouts** – Divide sections into equal columns to create a professional look.

Organizing with Layers

Wix allows you to manage layers, which is useful when working with overlapping elements.

- **Access Layers Panel** – Click on "Tools" and enable the "Layers" panel to see all elements stacked in your design.

- **Rearrange Elements** – Drag and drop elements in the layer list to move them forward or backward.

- **Lock Layers** – Prevent accidental changes by locking layers that shouldn't be moved.

Applying Effects

Wix provides various visual effects that can make your site more appealing:

- **Blur and Shadows** – Add depth to images and buttons.

- **Opacity Adjustments** – Make elements partially transparent for a stylish look.

- **Gradients and Overlays** – Use color gradients to add a modern touch to your backgrounds.

Customizing Mobile-Friendly Versions of Your Site

With more than half of all web traffic coming from mobile devices, having a mobile-optimized website is essential. Wix offers a dedicated mobile editor that allows you to customize your site's mobile version separately from the desktop layout.

Steps to Customize Your Mobile Site:

1. **Switch to Mobile View** – Click on the mobile icon in the top menu of the Wix Editor.

2. **Rearrange Elements** – Wix automatically adjusts your content for mobile, but you may need to tweak spacing and alignment.

3. **Hide Unnecessary Sections** – You can hide certain elements that don't work well on mobile (e.g., large images or complex animations).

4. **Optimize Buttons and Text** – Make sure buttons are large enough to be tapped easily and text is readable without zooming.

5. **Test Across Devices** – Preview your site on different screen sizes to ensure it looks great on all devices.

Mastering Wix's advanced design features can elevate your website to a professional level. By using Wix's AI tools, animations, grids, layers, and mobile customization options, you can create a site that is both visually stunning and user-friendly. Whether you are designing a business site, online store, or personal blog, these tools will help you craft a site that stands out in today's digital landscape.

Chapter 7: Branding Your Website for Maximum Impact

Choosing the Right Color Scheme and Fonts for Your Brand

Your website's color scheme and fonts are the first things visitors notice. They create a subconscious impression of your brand before a single word is read. Choosing the right colors and typography is crucial to establishing trust, professionalism, and brand identity.

Understanding Color Psychology in Branding

Each color evokes specific emotions and associations. Here's a breakdown of how colors influence perception:

- **Blue** – Trust, professionalism, reliability (used by brands like Facebook and LinkedIn).

- **Red** – Energy, passion, urgency (Coca-Cola, YouTube).

- **Green** – Growth, health, tranquility (Starbucks, Whole Foods).

- **Black** – Luxury, sophistication, power (Chanel, Apple).

47

- **Yellow** – Optimism, friendliness, attention-grabbing (McDonald's, IKEA).

When choosing a color scheme for your website, consider your brand message and target audience. Wix provides a **Color Picker Tool** and pre-made palettes to help you find a harmonious combination. Use a **primary color** for branding, **secondary colors** for accents, and a **neutral background** to maintain readability.

Selecting the Perfect Font Combination

Fonts contribute significantly to brand perception. There are three primary font categories:

1. **Serif Fonts** (Times New Roman, Georgia): Classic, traditional, professional.

2. **Sans-Serif Fonts** (Arial, Helvetica, Open Sans): Modern, clean, and easy to read.

3. **Script or Decorative Fonts** (Pacifico, Lobster): Stylish and unique, best used sparingly.

A **great combination** is pairing a bold sans-serif font for headings with a clean, readable serif font for body text. Wix allows you to customize fonts under the **Text Settings Panel** in the editor.

Creating a Professional Logo with Wix Logo Maker

A logo is the visual representation of your brand. If you don't have one, Wix offers a powerful **AI-based Logo Maker** to help create a custom design without needing a graphic designer.

How to Use Wix Logo Maker:

1. **Go to Wix Logo Maker** – Navigate to Wix's branding tools and select "Logo Maker."

2. **Enter Your Business Name** – Input your brand name and tagline (if applicable).

3. **Choose Your Style** – Wix will ask about your preferences (modern, playful, minimalist, etc.).

4. **Customize the Design** – Select colors, fonts, and icons that match your brand.

5. **Download Your Logo** – Once satisfied, purchase and download your logo in high resolution.

For consistency, apply your logo across all pages, including the **header, favicon, and email signatures**.

The Psychology of Website Design and User Experience (UX)

User experience (UX) directly affects engagement, conversion rates, and return visitors. If your website is confusing or unattractive, users will leave within seconds.

Key UX Principles for Branding Success

1. **Consistency** – Keep fonts, colors, and spacing uniform across all pages.

2. **Navigation Simplicity** – Limit your main menu to 5-7 items to reduce clutter.

3. **Whitespace** – Avoid overcrowding pages. White space improves readability and creates a professional look.

4. **Mobile Optimization** – Wix allows you to adjust elements for mobile viewing to ensure a seamless experience.

5. **Call-to-Action (CTA)** – Use strong CTAs like **"Get Started," "Book Now," or "Contact Us"** to guide users toward an action.

How to Make Your Website Look Professional Even Without a Designer

Hiring a designer isn't necessary when Wix provides professional tools to elevate your site's aesthetics. Here's how you can achieve a polished look on your own:

1. Use Wix's Pre-Designed Templates

Wix offers hundreds of industry-specific templates. Pick one that aligns with your business and customize it to fit your branding.

2. Keep Your Layout Clean

Avoid clutter. Stick to a **structured grid layout** using Wix's strip and section tools to organize content effectively.

3. High-Quality Images and Videos

- Use **Wix's Media Library** or high-resolution stock images from sites like Unsplash or Pexels.

- Optimize images for faster loading times using Wix's built-in **Image Resizer**.

4. Use Wix Design Features Like a Pro

- **Custom animations** – Apply fade-in effects for smooth transitions.

- **Overlays and opacity settings** – Make text more readable on images.

- **Shapes and icons** – Add elements for visual appeal without overcrowding.

5. Test and Preview Before Publishing

- Use **Wix's Preview Mode** to see how your website looks before going live.

- Get feedback from friends or potential customers for final adjustments.

Branding your Wix website doesn't require expensive designers—just the right tools and strategy. By selecting the perfect colors and fonts, designing a logo, prioritizing UX, and using Wix's built-in features, you can create a professional and impactful website that represents your brand effectively.

Chapter 8: SEO Optimization – Get Found on Google

Understanding Wix SEO Tools and How to Use Them

Search engine optimization (SEO) is the key to making your website visible on search engines like Google. Wix provides several built-in tools to help you optimize your site without requiring extensive technical knowledge.

Wix SEO Wiz

Wix SEO Wiz is a step-by-step guide designed to help website owners improve their search rankings. When you first set up your site, the tool asks a series of questions about your business and target audience. Based on your responses, it generates a personalized SEO plan that includes:

- Keyword recommendations

- Title and meta description optimization

- Mobile-friendliness checks

- Indexing status updates

To access Wix SEO Wiz:

1. Go to your **Wix Dashboard**.

2. Click on **Marketing & SEO**.

3. Select **SEO** and then **Get Found on Google**.

4. Follow the instructions provided to optimize your site.

Structured Data & Schema Markup

Wix allows you to add **structured data markup**, which helps search engines understand your content better. You can implement this in the **Advanced SEO Settings** under your page settings.

For example, if you run an online store, adding product schema markup can help your items appear in Google Shopping results.

Google Search Console Integration

Connecting your Wix site to **Google Search Console** allows you to track indexing status, fix errors, and gain insights into your site's search performance.

To connect:

1. Navigate to your Wix SEO Settings.

2. Click **Get Found on Google**.

3. Follow the instructions to verify your domain with Google.

How to Optimize Page Titles, Meta Descriptions, and Keywords

Your page titles and meta descriptions play a crucial role in SEO. They are what users see when your site appears in search results.

Optimizing Page Titles

A good **page title** should be:

- Between **50-60 characters**

- Include your primary keyword

- Be compelling to encourage clicks

Example: Instead of a generic title like *About Us*, use something more descriptive like *About [Your Business Name] – Quality [Your Niche] Services.*

Writing Effective Meta Descriptions

Your **meta description** should:

- Be **150-160 characters** long

- Summarize your page's content

- Include a call to action (e.g., *Learn More, Get Started Today*)

Example: *Looking for the best handmade jewelry? Explore our collection of artisan-crafted necklaces, rings, and more. Shop now!*

Keyword Optimization

Keyword placement matters. Here's where to include them:

- **Page titles and meta descriptions**
- **Headings (H1, H2, H3)**
- **Alt text for images**
- **URLs**
- **Body content (naturally, not stuffed)**

Use Wix's **SEO Patterns** to automatically apply SEO-friendly structures to multiple pages.

Speed Optimization: How to Make Your Wix Site Load Faster

Google considers **site speed** a ranking factor. A slow website can hurt both SEO and user experience. Here's how to optimize your Wix site's speed:

1. Optimize Images

Large images slow down your site. Follow these best practices:

- Use **JPEG** for photos and **PNG** for transparent images.

- Compress images using tools like **TinyPNG** before uploading.

- Set image width to **1200px or less** for optimal display.

2. Minimize the Use of Animations and Videos

While animations enhance aesthetics, too many can slow down your site. Keep them minimal, and use **lazy loading** for images and videos.

3. Enable Caching and CDN

Wix automatically applies **caching** and **Content Delivery Networks (CDN)** to load your site faster worldwide. Make sure to enable these settings in your **Performance Dashboard**.

4. Reduce the Number of Apps and Widgets

Some third-party apps slow down your site. Only install apps that are essential to your functionality.

5. Optimize Your Mobile Version

Google ranks mobile-friendly sites higher. To optimize:

- Use **Wix Mobile Editor** to adjust layouts.

- Ensure text is readable and buttons are easily clickable.

- Avoid pop-ups that interfere with navigation.

How to Rank Higher with Wix Blog and Content Marketing

Regularly publishing **high-quality content** is one of the best ways to rank higher on Google. Here's how you can leverage Wix's blogging features:

1. Set Up Your Wix Blog

1. In your Wix Dashboard, go to **Blog**.

2. Click **Create New Post**.

3. Add a compelling title, content, and SEO settings.

2. Use Long-Form, SEO-Optimized Content

Google favors **long, informative content** (1,000+ words). Ensure your blog posts:

- Answer common user questions

- Include relevant **keywords**

- Have **structured headings** (H1, H2, H3)

- Feature **internal links** to other pages on your site

3. Optimize Blog SEO Settings

Each blog post should have:

- A unique **title and meta description**

- A **custom URL** with relevant keywords

- Proper **image alt text**

4. Promote Your Blog for More Traffic

SEO alone isn't enough—you need to drive traffic through multiple channels:

- **Share on social media** (Facebook, LinkedIn, Twitter)

- **Engage in guest blogging** to earn backlinks

- **Use email marketing** to notify subscribers of new content

Mastering Wix SEO isn't just about making technical tweaks—it's about creating **valuable content** and ensuring a seamless **user experience**. By leveraging Wix SEO tools, optimizing your site's structure, improving loading speed, and utilizing content marketing, you can significantly boost your rankings and drive more traffic to your website.

The next chapter will explore **monetization strategies**, showing you how to turn your Wix website into a profitable business!

Chapter 9: Setting Up an Online Store with Wix E-Commerce

Thanks to Wix E-Commerce, creating an online store has never been easier. Whether selling handmade crafts or digital products or running a full-scale online retail business, Wix provides the tools to launch, manage, and grow your store successfully. This chapter walks you through setting up a profitable online store using Wix E-Commerce.

Choosing the Best Wix E-Commerce Plan

Wix offers multiple pricing plans, but not all include e-commerce capabilities. Selecting the right plan before launching your online store is crucial to unlocking essential features such as payment processing, unlimited products, and advanced analytics.

Wix E-Commerce Plans:

1. **Business Basic**—This plan is ideal for startups and small sellers. It includes secure online payments, unlimited products, abandoned cart recovery, and selling on social media.

2. **Business Unlimited**—This plan is perfect for growing businesses. In addition to the features in Business Basic, it includes subscription services, automated sales tax (for up to 100 transactions per month), and advanced shipping tools.

3. **Business VIP** – Best for scaling and professional sellers. It offers priority customer support, unlimited automated sales tax calculations, and loyalty program integrations.

Which Plan Should You Choose?

If you're starting, the **Business Basic** plan may be sufficient. However, if you need features like dropshipping, automated tax calculations, or advanced marketing tools, consider upgrading to **Business Unlimited** or **VIP**. Investing in the right plan ensures seamless scaling as your store grows.

How to Add Products and Set Up Payment Methods

Once you've chosen your Wix E-Commerce plan, you can start adding products and configuring payment settings.

Step 1: Adding Products

1. **Go to Wix Dashboard** → Click on **Store Products**.

2. **Click "+ Add a Product"** and select the type (physical, digital, or service).

3. **Upload High-Quality Images** – Use at least 3–5 images per product from different angles.

4. **Write a Compelling Product Title and Description** – Clearly describe the product's features, benefits, and specifications.

5. **Set the Price** – Ensure competitive pricing based on market research.

6. **Manage Inventory and Variations**—If you offer different sizes, colors, or styles, you must configure product variations.

7. **Click Save & Publish** – Your product is now live on your Wix store.

Step 2: Setting Up Payment Methods

To accept payments, you need to connect to a payment provider.

1. **Go to Settings** → Click **Accept Payments**.

2. Choose from multiple payment options:

   o **Wix Payments** – You can accept credit/debit cards and Apple Pay with low transaction fees.

   o **PayPal** – A widely used global payment gateway.

   o **Stripe/Square** – Ideal for businesses wanting multiple processing options.

   o **Manual Payments** – Accept cash or bank transfers for offline purchases.

3. Complete the setup and test transactions to ensure smooth customer checkout experiences.

Designing a High-Converting Product Page

Your product page plays a crucial role in turning visitors into paying customers. A well-optimized product page enhances user experience and encourages conversions.

Essential Elements of a Product Page:

1. **Clear and Engaging Product Titles** – Keep them short and informative.

Mega Jammy

2. **High-Quality Images & Videos** – Show the product from multiple angles.

3. **Compelling Product Descriptions** – Highlight key benefits and use bullet points for readability.

4. **Pricing and Discounts** – Show original vs. discounted prices if applicable.

5. **Call-to-Action (CTA) Buttons** – Use "Add to Cart" or "Buy Now" buttons that stand out.

6. **Customer Reviews and Ratings** – Social proof increases trust.

7. **Shipping & Return Policy** – State delivery times and return conditions.

Best Practices:

- Use **Urgency & Scarcity** (e.g., "Limited Stock Available").

- Offer **Bundle Deals** or **Related Products** to increase sales.

- Optimize for **Mobile Users** – Ensure your product page looks great on smaller screens.

How to Handle Shipping, Taxes, and Customer Support

Managing logistics effectively ensures smooth operations and customer satisfaction. Here's how to configure shipping, taxes, and customer support in your Wix store.

Step 1: Setting Up Shipping

1. **Go to Settings** → Select **Shipping & Fulfillment**.

2. Choose your shipping region (local or international).

3. Set up shipping rates:

   - **Flat Rate** – Charge a fixed shipping fee per order.

   - **Weight-Based** – Fees depend on package weight.

   - **Free Shipping** – Encourages more purchases.

   - **Real-Time Carrier Rates** – Use carriers like FedEx, USPS, or DHL.

4. Configure delivery times and tracking options.

66

5. Save and apply changes to all products or specific categories.

Step 2: Configuring Taxes

1. **Go to Settings** → Click **Tax Settings**.

2. Enable **Automated Sales Tax** (available in Business Unlimited and VIP plans).

3. Set up tax rules based on country and region.

4. If selling internationally, check compliance with VAT or GST regulations.

Step 3: Managing Customer Support

Happy customers are repeat customers. Provide excellent support using Wix's built-in tools.

- **Live Chat** – Activate Wix Chat to assist customers in real-time.

- **FAQ Page** – Answer common queries to reduce inquiries.

- **Return & Refund Policies** – Make them clear and accessible.

- **Email & Ticket Support** – Use Wix's CRM tools to handle queries professionally.

- **Integrate Help Desk Apps** – Consider third-party apps like Zendesk for better customer support management.

Setting up a successful online store with Wix E-Commerce requires careful planning and execution. Choosing the right plan, effectively adding products, optimizing product pages, and managing shipping, taxes, and customer support is critical to building a profitable online business. Wix simplifies the process with its user-friendly interface, making it accessible for beginners and experienced entrepreneurs. These steps will create a seamless customer shopping experience and position your store for long-term success.

Chapter 10: Using Wix for Service-Based Businesses & Blogs

How to Set Up Wix Bookings for Appointments and Services

Wix Bookings is a powerful tool designed to help service-based businesses manage their schedules and offer seamless appointment bookings online. Whether you run a salon, a coaching business, or a fitness training service, Wix Bookings simplifies scheduling appointments and collecting payments.

Step 1: Adding Wix Bookings to Your Site

1. **Access the Wix Editor** – Access your website and navigate the **App Market**.

2. **Search for "Wix Bookings"** – Click "Add to Site" and wait for the integration to complete.

3. **Set Up Your Booking Services** – Open the Wix Dashboard, click "Bookings," and click "Add New Service."

4. **Define Service Details** – Enter details such as the service name, duration, price, and availability.

5. **Customize Your Booking Page** – Design the booking page layout, ensuring it aligns with your brand.

6. **Enable Online Payments** – Connect your payment methods through Wix Payments, PayPal, or Stripe to accept payments upfront.

7. **Test the Booking Flow** – Run a test appointment to ensure a smooth user experience before launching.

Benefits of Wix Bookings:

- Automated email reminders for clients.

- Calendar synchronization with Google Calendar.

- The ability to set recurring appointments and group sessions.

- Mobile-friendly booking for clients on the go.

Creating a Membership or Subscription Website with Wix

If you want to offer exclusive content, coaching programs, or community access, Wix's membership feature allows you to create a subscription-based website with different pricing tiers.

Step 1: Enable Membership Feature

1. **Navigate to the Dashboard** – Go to "Settings" and enable "Member's Area."

2. **Customize Member Pages** – Design pages that only registered users can access.

3. **Add Subscription Plans** – Install the "Wix Pricing Plans" app and create multiple membership levels.

4. **Set Up Payment Options** – Choose a one-time payment, recurring billing, or free trial option.

5. **Launch and Promote** – Encourage sign-ups through email campaigns, social media, and discount offers.

Examples of Membership Websites

- **Online courses** – Offer exclusive video tutorials for paying members.

- **Fitness programs** – Provide premium workout plans and nutrition guides.

- **VIP business networking groups** – Give members access to special webinars and resources.

Blogging with Wix: How to Write and Optimize Blog Posts

A well-maintained blog can drive organic traffic to your website and position you as an expert. Wix offers a feature-rich blogging tool that makes content creation simple.

Step 1: Adding a Blog to Your Wix Site

1. **Go to the Wix Editor** – Click "Add Apps" and search for "Wix Blog."

2. **Set Up Blog Categories** – Organize your content into relevant topics for easier navigation.

3. **Customize the Blog Layout** – Choose from Wix's pre-designed templates or modify them to match your branding.

4. **Create Your First Post** – Click "New Post," and add a catchy title, engaging content, and high-quality images.

5. **SEO Optimization** – Optimize the post title, meta description, and image alt texts to improve search rankings.

Blogging Best Practices

- Use **compelling headlines** to grab attention.

- Add **internal and external links** to boost credibility and engagement.

- **Include a call to action (CTA)** to encourage readers to subscribe or purchase a service.

- Optimize content for readability with **short paragraphs and bullet points**.

How to Use Wix Email Marketing to Grow Your Audience

Email marketing remains one of the most effective ways to nurture leads and retain customers. Wix Email Marketing (ShoutOut) allows you to send newsletters, promotions, and automated follow-ups.

Step 1: Setting Up Wix Email Marketing

1. **Go to the Wix Dashboard** – Navigate to "Marketing & SEO" and select "Email Marketing."

2. **Choose a Template** – Use Wix's pre-designed email templates or create your own.

3. **Add Engaging Content** – Write compelling subject lines, include high-quality images, and add CTA buttons.

4. **Segment Your Audience** – Create email lists for new subscribers, existing customers, and VIP members.

5. **Schedule and Send** – Preview your email, choose a delivery time, and hit send.

6. **Track Performance** – Use Wix's analytics to monitor open rates, clicks, and conversions.

Email Marketing Tips:

- **Personalize Your Emails** – Address subscribers by name and tailor content based on their interests.

- **Use Automated Responses** – Set up autoresponders for new sign-ups and abandoned carts.

- **Test Subject Lines** – A/B test different subject lines to see which generates higher open rates.

Wix offers a range of tools to help service-based businesses and bloggers thrive online. You can effectively grow your brand and increase revenue by leveraging Wix Bookings, setting up membership plans, optimizing blog posts, and using email marketing. Take advantage of these features to create a professional, engaging, and profitable online presence.

Chapter 11: AI, Automation, and Wix Apps

How to Use Wix's AI for Smart Website Creation

Wix has revolutionized website creation with AI-powered tools, making building a professional-looking site in minutes easier than ever. If you don't have the time or expertise to design a site from scratch, Wix ADI (Artificial Design Intelligence) can do most of the heavy lifting for you.

Step-by-Step Guide to Using Wix ADI:

1. **Getting Started:** When you sign up for Wix, you'll be given two options: create a site using Wix Editor or let Wix ADI build one.

2. **Answering Questions:** Wix ADI asks simple questions about your business type, industry, and preferences. Based on your responses, it selects the most suitable templates, layouts, and features.

3. **AI-Generated Design:** Wix ADI generates a complete website with images, text, and color schemes tailored to your brand.

76

4. **Customization:** While the AI does most of the work, you can tweak elements, change fonts, update colors, and refine layouts to match your vision.

5. **Publishing:** Once you are satisfied with the design, hit "Publish," and your site will go live instantly.

Benefits of Using Wix AI:

- **Time-saving:** The AI-powered process reduces the time spent on manual design.

- **Personalization:** The AI selects layouts and colors that align with your industry.

- **Easy Edits:** You can fine-tune everything manually if needed.

For those who want more control over their design but still want AI assistance, Wix offers the Wix Editor with AI-driven suggestions, helping you create a custom site without needing coding skills.

Best Wix Apps for Business, Marketing, and Growth

Wix has an extensive App Market with tools designed to enhance functionality, boost engagement, and drive sales. Below are some must-have apps to grow your online presence:

Marketing & SEO Apps

1. **Wix SEO Wiz:** This built-in tool helps you optimize your site for search engines by providing step-by-step guidance on keywords, meta descriptions, and indexing.

2. **Visitor Analytics:** This tool tracks site visitors, user behavior, and conversion rates to help you improve your website's performance.

3. **Get Google Ads:** This feature enables you to create and manage Google Ads directly from Wix, helping to increase traffic and conversions.

E-Commerce & Business Management Apps

4. **Wix Stores:** A robust solution for setting up an online store, managing inventory, and processing payments.

78

5. **Printful:** You can sell custom-designed products without managing inventory, as orders are printed and shipped on demand.

6. **Wix Bookings:** Perfect for service-based businesses, this app lets customers book appointments and pay online.

Engagement & Customer Support Apps

7. **Wix Chat:** Enables real-time customer interaction, increasing engagement and potential sales.

8. **Tidio Live Chat:** A powerful chatbot that helps automate responses and improve customer service.

9. **Social Media Stream:** Displays live social media feeds on your website, keeping visitors engaged.

Adding these apps to your Wix site can dramatically enhance user experience, automate tasks, and scale your business effectively.

Automating Your Website with Wix Workflows

Automation is key to streamlining operations and ensuring your website runs smoothly without constant manual intervention. Wix Workflows is an advanced feature designed to automate tasks and improve business efficiency.

How to Set Up Wix Workflows

1. **Access Wix Workflows:** Navigate to your Wix dashboard and select 'Automation' under the settings.

2. **Choose a Trigger:** A trigger is an action that starts an automation, such as submitting a new contact form.

3. **Select an Action:** This response to the trigger, such as sending an automated email or adding a new subscriber to your mailing list.

4. **Customize Conditions:** Define rules, such as sending a follow-up email only if the customer hasn't responded within 48 hours.

5. **Activate and Monitor:** Turn on the automation and track its performance.

Common Wix Workflow Automation

- **Lead Capture Follow-Ups:** Automatically send a welcome email when a visitor subscribes.

- **Abandoned Cart Recovery:** Send reminders to users who left items in their cart.

- **Appointment Confirmations:** Instantly notify clients when they book a service.

- **Customer Engagement:** Automatically post a thank-you message after a purchase.

By setting up this automation, you can effortlessly save time, reduce human error, and enhance customer interactions.

Integrating Wix with Social Media and Other Platforms

Social media and third-party integrations can significantly boost your website's visibility, engagement, and functionality. Wix easily connects your site with platforms like Facebook, Instagram, Google Analytics, and more.

How to Connect Social Media to Wix

1. **Add Social Icons:** Use Wix's built-in social media buttons to link your profiles to your site.

2. **Embed Social Feeds:** Use apps like 'Social Media Stream' to display real-time posts from Instagram or Twitter.

3. **Enable Social Sharing:** Allow visitors to share your content directly to their social networks.

4. **Run Facebook and Instagram Ads:** Sync your Wix site with Facebook Pixel to track ad performance and retarget visitors.

Third-Party Platform Integrations

- **Google Analytics:** Tracks website traffic, visitor behavior, and conversion rates.

- **Mailchimp & Wix Email Marketing:** Helps manage email campaigns and customer engagement.

- **Zapier:** Automates tasks by connecting Wix with hundreds of other apps.

- **Stripe & PayPal:** Integrates secure payment processing options for e-commerce businesses.

Benefits of Social and Third-Party Integrations

- **Increases Traffic:** Social media connections drive more visitors to your site.

- **Boosts Engagement:** Live feeds and interactive elements keep users engaged.

- **Enhances Marketing:** Third-party tools help optimize SEO, email marketing, and advertising strategies.

Mastering Wix's AI, automation tools, and app integrations can take your website to the next level. Whether you're streamlining your workflow, optimizing marketing efforts, or improving customer engagement, Wix provides the features to make your website functional and highly effective. By leveraging these advanced tools, you can automate tedious tasks, increase conversions, and focus more on growing your business.

If you're ready to harness the full power of Wix, start implementing these strategies today and watch your website thrive!

Chapter 12: Common Mistakes to Avoid When Designing Your Wix Site

Why Your Wix Site Might Look Unprofessional (And How to Fix It)

Creating a website on Wix is a straightforward process, but small design mistakes can make your site look unpolished or amateurish. Here are some common pitfalls and how to correct them:

1. Inconsistent Fonts and Colors

A cohesive brand identity is essential for professionalism. Using multiple font styles or an inconsistent color scheme makes your site look chaotic. Stick to:

- **A maximum of two to three fonts** (one for headings, one for body text, and an optional accent font).

- **A color palette** of no more than five complementary colors. Wix provides built-in color schemes to help you maintain harmony.

2. Cluttered Layout and Poor Spacing

Overloading a page with text, images, and buttons can be overwhelming. Use **white space** strategically to improve readability and guide users' focus.

- Ensure adequate padding and margins between sections.

- Use **grids and columns** in Wix's editor to create a well-structured layout.

- Keep important information **above the fold** (visible without scrolling) for immediate engagement.

3. Low-Quality Images or Unoptimized Media

Blurry or pixelated images lower your website's credibility. Always optimize high-resolution images for the web to maintain fast loading speeds.

- Use Wix's **built-in media tools** to compress and resize images.

- Stick to **WebP or optimized JPEG formats** for the best balance of quality and performance.

- Avoid auto-playing videos unless necessary to prevent slow loading.

4. Lack of Mobile Optimization

A mobile-friendly site is essential, as over 50% of web traffic comes from mobile devices.

- Use **Wix's mobile editor** to adjust layouts for smaller screens.

- Check that buttons and text are readable and clickable.

- Avoid large blocks of text that require excessive scrolling.

5. Missing Call-to-Action (CTA)

A clear CTA guides visitors toward the next step (buying, signing up, or contacting you). Ensure each page includes an engaging CTA with the following:

- **Strong action words** (e.g., "Get Started," "Shop Now").

- **Visible placement**, preferably above the fold.

- **Contrasting colors** to stand out.

The Most Overlooked SEO Mistakes and How to Correct Them

Even a beautifully designed website won't perform well if it's not optimized for search engines. Here's what you might be missing:

1. Ignoring Page Titles and Meta Descriptions

Each page needs a unique **title tag and meta description** to improve search rankings.

- Go to **SEO settings** in Wix and customize each page's title and description.

- Include **primary keywords** naturally (e.g., "Best Handmade Jewelry | Buy Unique Designs Online").

- Keep descriptions under **160 characters** to avoid truncation in search results.

2. Not Using Header Tags (H1, H2, H3)

Search engines use headers to understand page structure. Optimize by:

- Having **one H1 tag per page** (usually the page title).

88

- Using H2 and H3 tags for **subsections** to improve readability.

- Ensuring header tags include relevant keywords naturally.

3. Slow Loading Speeds Due to Unoptimized Content

Speed affects both **user experience and SEO rankings**. Wix offers tools to enhance performance:

- **Enable Wix's site optimization** settings.

- **Limit large images and videos** or use lazy loading.

- **Reduce excessive animations** and third-party apps.

- **Use Wix's built-in caching** for faster load times.

4. Lack of Internal and External Links

Internal linking helps search engines and users navigate your site.

- Link to relevant pages within your site (e.g., from a blog post to a product page).

- Ensure all links open in a **new tab** if they lead to external websites.

- Avoid broken links by regularly testing them with Wix's **SEO audit tool**.

5. Not Submitting Your Sitemap to Google

Wix automatically creates a sitemap, but you must **submit it manually in Google Search Console** for faster indexing.

- Go to **Wix SEO settings** and copy your sitemap URL.

- Submit it under the **Sitemaps** section in Google Search Console.

Why Your Wix Store Isn't Selling and How to Improve It

Running an online store through Wix is convenient, but without the right strategies, sales may remain low. Let's fix that:

1. Poor Product Descriptions and Images

Customers rely on product descriptions and images to make decisions. Improve them by:

Mega Jammy

- Using **detailed and benefit-driven descriptions** (e.g., "Soft, breathable cotton T-shirt perfect for all-day comfort.").

- Including **high-quality images** from multiple angles.

- Adding **zoom and video features** for an enhanced shopping experience.

2. Confusing Checkout Process

A complicated checkout process increases cart abandonment.

- Enable **guest checkout** to avoid forcing account creation.

- Offer multiple payment options like **credit/debit cards, PayPal, and digital wallets**.

- Use a **progress bar** to show customers how close they are to completing their purchase.

3. Hidden Shipping Costs

Unexpected fees lead to cart abandonment.

- Display **clear shipping costs** upfront.

- Offer **free shipping thresholds** (e.g., "Free shipping on orders over $50").

- Use **Wix's shipping calculator** to provide accurate estimates.

4. Lack of Customer Trust Signals

People won't buy from a store they don't trust. Increase credibility by:

- Displaying **customer reviews and testimonials**.

- Showing **secure payment badges** (e.g., SSL encryption, PayPal security).

- Including **a clear return policy** on product pages.

5. Not Using Email Marketing to Retarget Visitors

Many visitors leave without purchasing. Bring them back through:

- **Abandoned cart emails** reminding them of their pending order.

- **Discount offers** to encourage a first-time purchase.

- **Loyalty rewards** for repeat customers.

A successful Wix website is more than just a visually appealing design—it requires proper SEO, strong branding, user-friendly navigation, and optimized e-commerce features. By avoiding these common mistakes and applying the solutions above, you can create a high-performing website that attracts visitors, ranks well on search engines, and converts traffic into sales. If your Wix site isn't delivering the expected results, review these areas and implement the recommended fixes. The right adjustments can make all the difference in turning a struggling site into a thriving online presence.

Chapter 13: Troubleshooting and Fixing Issues
How to Fix Slow-Loading Wix Websites

A slow-loading website is frustrating for visitors and can negatively impact SEO rankings. If your Wix site is taking too long to load, here are some practical steps to speed it up:

Optimize Images and Media Files

Large image and video files can be a major reason behind slow site speed. To fix this:

- Compress images before uploading using tools like TinyPNG or ImageOptim.

- Use the correct file format: JPEGs for photos, PNGs for transparent images, and WebP for modern compression.

- Avoid using unnecessarily high-resolution images.

- Enable Wix's built-in image optimization, which automatically compresses media files for better performance.

Reduce the Number of Apps and Widgets

While Wix offers a wide range of apps, having too many can slow down your website. Uninstall any apps that are not essential for your business.

Use Fewer Fonts and Animations

Excessive custom fonts and animations can cause performance issues. Stick to two or three fonts and minimize using complex animations, parallax effects, and video backgrounds.

Enable Caching and Lazy Loading

Wix automatically caches pages, but you can enhance this by using:

- Lazy loading for images, so they only load when users scroll to them.

- Fewer dynamic elements like live chat widgets and embedded social media feeds.

Minimize the Use of Heavy Third-Party Code

External scripts, such as analytics trackers and custom code, can slow down your site. Ensure only necessary scripts are added and use asynchronous loading whenever possible.

Check Your Hosting Plan

Although Wix provides reliable hosting, if your website has high traffic and complex functionalities, consider upgrading to a premium plan with better performance features.

What to Do If Your Wix Site Is Not Ranking on Google

If your Wix website isn't appearing on Google search results, there are several potential reasons and solutions:

Ensure Your Site Is Indexed

- Go to Google Search Console and check if your site is indexed by typing site:yourdomain.com into Google.

- If your site isn't indexed, manually submit your sitemap through Google Search Console.

- Make sure your site is set to "visible" in Wix's SEO settings.

Improve Your SEO Settings

Mega Jammy

Wix provides built-in SEO tools to help optimize your website for search engines:

- Customize page titles and meta descriptions with relevant keywords.

- Use Wix's SEO Wiz tool to follow step-by-step optimization suggestions.

- Implement keyword-rich headers and content throughout your pages.

Optimize Content for SEO

Google prioritizes websites with high-quality content. To enhance your SEO:

- Create valuable blog posts and landing pages with targeted keywords.

- Internal linking is used to guide users and help search engines understand site structure.

- Ensure each page has unique, well-written content to avoid duplication.

Improve Mobile Friendliness

Google ranks mobile-friendly websites higher in search results. Ensure:

- Your site is fully responsive (use Wix's mobile editor to adjust layouts).

- Fonts are readable, buttons are easy to click, and navigation is user-friendly.

Increase Backlinks and Social Signals

- Build high-quality backlinks by getting featured on industry blogs and directories.

- Share your content on social media and encourage engagement.

Check for Technical SEO Errors

Use SEO audit tools like Google Search Console or Ahrefs to detect technical SEO problems such as broken links, missing alt text, or duplicate content.

Fixing Mobile Responsiveness Issues

Many visitors browse websites from their smartphones, so ensuring your Wix site looks good on mobile devices is crucial. If your site has display issues on mobile, follow these steps:

Use Wix's Mobile Editor

Mega Jammy

Wix provides a separate mobile editor to fine-tune how your site appears on mobile devices:

- Adjust text sizes, button placements, and images to fit smaller screens.

- Hide unnecessary elements that don't enhance the mobile experience.

Enable Mobile-Friendly Features

- Activate Wix's automatic mobile optimization.

- Use flexible layouts to prevent elements from being cut off on smaller screens.

- Ensure call-to-action buttons are large enough to be easily tapped.

Reduce Heavy Content on Mobile

- Avoid using long paragraphs; break text into shorter, easy-to-read sections.

- Limit the number of high-resolution images and videos.

- Simplify navigation by using dropdown menus or hamburger icons.

Test Your Site on Different Devices

Mega Jammy

- Use Wix's built-in mobile preview mode.

- Manually test on various smartphones and tablets to check how the site responds.

- Run a mobile-friendly test using Google's Mobile Test Tool.

Fix Touchscreen Navigation Issues

If users struggle to navigate your site on mobile, check the following:

- The buttons and links should be spaced properly (minimum 48px apart).

- Forms are easy to fill out and don't require excessive scrolling.

- There are no hover effects that don't translate well to touchscreens.

Addressing these issues can ensure a faster, more visible, and mobile-friendly Wix site, leading to a better user experience and improved search engine performance.

Chapter 14: Real-World Case Studies – Successful Wix Websites

Case Study #1: A Small Business That Thrived with Wix

Background:

A passionate baker, Sarah had been selling homemade cakes and pastries from her home kitchen for years. While she had a loyal local customer base, she struggled to expand her business beyond word-of-mouth referrals. She knew she needed an online presence but had little technical expertise and a limited budget for web development. That's when she discovered Wix.

How Wix Helped:

Sarah used Wix's intuitive drag-and-drop editor to design a professional website without writing a single line of code. She selected a pre-designed bakery template and customized it to reflect her brand colors and aesthetics.

- **Wix E-Commerce Integration**: She set up an online store using Wix Stores, enabling

101

customers to place orders directly from her website.

- **Booking Feature**: Using Wix Bookings, she allowed customers to schedule cake-tasting appointments.

- **SEO Tools**: Sarah utilized Wix's built-in SEO Wiz to optimize her site for search engines, ensuring her bakery appeared in local search results.

- **Social Media Integration**: She connected her Instagram feed to her site, showcasing her latest creations in real time.

- **Email Marketing**: With Wix Email Marketing, she launched newsletters and promotions for holiday specials and discounts.

Results:

Sarah's online sales tripled within six months of launching her Wix website. She started receiving orders from neighboring towns, expanded her business, and eventually opened a small storefront. Her website became the backbone of her bakery's success.

Case Study #2: A Personal Blog That Gained Massive Traffic

Background:

David, a freelance writer and travel enthusiast, had always wanted to start a travel blog. He needed a website that could handle high-quality images, blog posts, and video content while being mobile-friendly and easy to navigate. He opted for Wix to build his platform.

How Wix Helped:

- **Wix Blog**: David set up a blog using Wix's blogging platform, which allowed him to categorize content, add featured images, and create an engaging user experience.

- **SEO and Readability Enhancements**: Wix provided SEO suggestions, helping him optimize meta descriptions and keywords for better Google rankings.

- **Mobile Optimization**: Wix's automatic mobile responsiveness made his blog look great on smartphones and tablets.

- **Content Monetization**: He added Google AdSense and affiliate marketing links to monetize his blog.

- **Newsletter Subscription**: Using Wix Forms, he built an email list and sent weekly travel updates to subscribers.

Results:

Within a year, David's blog gained over 100,000 monthly visitors. His content was ranking on Google's first page for various travel keywords. He began earning a full-time income from blogging thanks to his monetization strategies.

Case Study #3: An E-Commerce Store That Increased Sales with Wix

Background:

Emma owned a small handmade jewelry business. Initially, she sold her products through social media, but keeping track of orders and customer messages became overwhelming. She needed a streamlined, professional e-commerce website and turned to Wix for a solution.

How Wix Helped:

- **Wix Stores**: She built an online store with an easy-to-use checkout process, multiple payment options, and automated order tracking.

- **Product Customization Options**: She used Wix's product pages to allow customers to choose different sizes, colors, and engraving options.

- **Abandoned Cart Recovery**: Wix automatically sent reminder emails to shoppers who left items in their cart, increasing conversions.

- **Integrated Marketing Tools**: She used Wix Email Marketing and Facebook Ads integration to drive more traffic to her store.

- **Customer Reviews**: With Wix's built-in review system, happy customers left testimonials that boosted her brand credibility.

Results:

Emma's sales doubled within three months. Her website provided a seamless shopping experience, increasing customer retention and loyalty. She eventually expanded her business to include wholesale partnerships, all thanks to the strong foundation Wix provided.

These real-world success stories highlight how Wix can empower small businesses, bloggers, and e-commerce entrepreneurs to achieve remarkable growth. Whether starting from scratch or upgrading an existing online presence, Wix provides the tools to succeed in today's digital landscape.

Chapter 15a: Final Steps to Website Success

How to Maintain and Update Your Wix Site Regularly

Once your Wix website is live, the work doesn't stop there. Keeping your site fresh, functional, and engaging requires ongoing maintenance and updates. A neglected website can lead to outdated information, broken links, security vulnerabilities, and a drop in search engine rankings. Here's how to stay on top of it:

1. Regular Content Updates

- **Refresh Blog Posts:** Keep your content relevant by updating old blog posts with new data, improved SEO, and fresh insights.

- **Update Business Information:** If your contact details, services, or pricing change, ensure your site reflects the latest updates.

- **Add New Content:** Whether it's new pages, blog posts, testimonials, or portfolio pieces, fresh content keeps visitors engaged and improves SEO.

2. Monitor and Improve Performance

- **Check Loading Speed:** Slow websites drive visitors away. Use the Wix Performance Dashboard to analyze and fix speed issues.

- **Fix Broken Links:** Use tools like Google Search Console to identify and repair broken links that harm your user experience and SEO.

- **Optimize Images:** Large, uncompressed images can slow your site down. Use Wix's built-in image optimization tools or external services like TinyPNG.

3. Security and Backup Measures

- **Enable HTTPS:** Wix provides SSL certificates, but ensure your site remains secure by regularly checking settings.

- **Backup Your Website:** Wix automatically saves versions of your site, but it's good practice to save important changes manually.

- **Monitor for Malware or Unwanted Content:** Monitor third-party integrations to avoid security risks.

4. Test Mobile Responsiveness

A significant portion of website traffic comes from mobile devices. Check your site's appearance and functionality on different screen sizes using Wix's Mobile Editor. Adjust fonts, button sizes, and layouts to ensure a seamless experience for mobile users.

The Best Wix Tools and Resources to Keep Improving Your Website

Wix offers a variety of built-in tools and third-party apps to help you improve your website's functionality, design, and user experience. Let's explore some of the most valuable resources:

1. Wix SEO Tools

- **SEO Wiz:** A step-by-step guide to optimizing your site for search engines.

- **Site Booster:** Helps improve your site's visibility on search engines and directories.

- **Google Search Console Integration:** You can track your site's appearance in search results and fix indexing issues.

2. Marketing and Engagement Tools

- **Wix Email Marketing:** Build and manage email campaigns to keep your audience engaged.

- **Social Media Integrations:** Connect your site to platforms like Facebook, Instagram, and LinkedIn to boost traffic.

- **Wix Chat and Forms:** Engage visitors in real time and collect important customer data.

3. Analytics and Performance Tracking

- **Wix Analytics Dashboard:** Provides insights into visitor behavior, traffic sources, and engagement metrics.

- **Google Analytics Integration:** A must-have for detailed tracking and data analysis.

- **Heatmaps (via third-party apps like Hotjar):** See how users interact with your site and identify areas for improvement.

4. Design and Customization Tools

- **Velo by Wix:** A developer-friendly tool for adding custom features to your website.

Mega Jammy

- **Wix App Market:** Offers hundreds of apps to extend your site's functionality.

- **Wix Ascend:** A full suite of marketing and automation tools for growing your business.

Final Tips for Long-Term Growth and Success

Building a successful Wix website is more than just a one-time effort. Long-term success requires continuous improvement, adaptability, and strategic planning. Here are some final tips to ensure your website remains effective and grows over time:

1. Keep User Experience (UX) a Priority

- **Simplify Navigation:** Make it easy for users to find what they want.

- **Improve Readability:** Use clear fonts, ample white space, and structured content.

- **Enhance Call-to-Actions (CTAs):** Use action-driven buttons to guide users toward desired actions.

2. Invest in SEO and Content Marketing

111

- **Optimize for Voice Search:** With smart assistants becoming more common, tailor content for voice search queries.

- **Target Long-Tail Keywords:** These phrases attract highly targeted traffic.

- **Leverage Video Content:** Wix Video allows you to host and monetize video content, a powerful engagement tool.

3. Build and Engage Your Audience

- **Create a Community:** A membership area or forum can help retain visitors.

- **Offer Lead Magnets:** Free resources like eBooks, webinars, or discounts encourage sign-ups.

- **Be Active on Social Media:** Share updates, engage with your audience, and drive traffic to your site.

4. Stay Updated with Wix Features

Wix regularly updates its platform with new features. Stay informed by:

- Reading the **Wix Blog** for the latest updates.

- Joining the **Wix Community Forum** to learn from other users.

- Follow Wix on **social media and newsletters** to stay ahead of new trends.

5. Test and Adapt Your Strategies

What works today might not work tomorrow. To achieve continuous improvement, regularly test different strategies, analyze data, and tweak your approach.

A Wix website isn't just a one-time project—it's an evolving platform that can grow with your business. By maintaining and updating your site regularly, leveraging the best tools available, and following long-term success strategies, you can ensure that your Wix site remains effective, engaging, and profitable for years.

BONUS CHAPTER: EXPERT TIPS & FREE RESOURCES

Free Tools and Websites to Help with Design, SEO, and Marketing

Building a successful website on Wix isn't just about using the platform's built-in features. You'll need to leverage free external tools that enhance design, improve SEO, and streamline marketing efforts to stand out. Here's a list of some of the best free resources to complement your Wix site:

1. Free Design Tools

- **Canva** – Ideal for creating professional-quality graphics, banners, and social media content.

- **Pexels & Unsplash** – Free stock photo websites with high-quality images you can legally use.

- **Coolors.co** – A free color palette generator to help you choose the perfect brand colors.

- **Figma** – A great tool for designing website mockups before applying them to your Wix site.

- **Remove.bg** – Automatically removes image backgrounds, allowing you to create clean, transparent visuals.

2. Free SEO Tools

- **Google Search Console** – Helps monitor your site's performance and identify SEO issues.

- **Ubersuggest** – Provides free keyword research and SEO insights.

- **AnswerThePublic** – Generates content ideas based on what people search online.

- **Yoast Real-Time Content Analysis** – Evaluates your page's readability and SEO friendliness.

3. Free Marketing Tools

- **Mailchimp (Free Plan)** – Email marketing software that integrates well with Wix.

- **Hootsuite (Free Plan)** – Schedules and manages social media posts across platforms.

- **Google Analytics** – Tracks website traffic and visitor behavior to optimize marketing strategies.

- **Trello** – Helps plan and organize content marketing efforts with a simple drag-and-drop interface.

Using these tools in combination with Wix's built-in features can significantly enhance your website's effectiveness, branding, and visibility online.

Wix Updates & How to Stay Ahead of Changes

Wix is constantly evolving with new features, AI-powered tools, and performance enhancements. To ensure your website stays up to date and benefits from these improvements, here's how you can keep up with Wix's latest updates:

1. Follow Wix's Official Channels

- **Wix Blog** (www.wix.com/blog) – Regularly shares platform updates, best practices, and design tips.

- **Wix YouTube Channel** – Features tutorials and walkthroughs of new features.

116

- **Wix Facebook and Twitter** – Provides real-time news and updates from the company.

2. Join the Wix Community

- **Wix Forum** – A space where Wix users share insights, ask questions, and discuss updates.

- **Wix Marketplace** – Connects you with Wix experts who can provide additional guidance.

- **Wix Partner Program** – If you're a designer or developer, you can gain early access to new tools.

3. Check for New Features in Your Wix Dashboard

Wix frequently rolls out updates that may not be widely advertised. Make it a habit to:

- Explore the **"What's New"** section in your dashboard.

- Test new beta features that Wix offers to select users.

- Regularly review your site settings to enable newly released tools.

4. Stay Informed About SEO & Algorithm Changes

Search engines like Google update their algorithms frequently, which can impact how your Wix site ranks. To stay ahead:

- Subscribe to SEO news websites like Moz, Search Engine Journal, and Google's official blog.

- Use tools like **Google Search Console** to monitor your site's indexing and search performance.

- Update your content regularly to align with current best practices.

By proactively keeping up with Wix updates, you ensure that your website remains competitive and benefits from the latest technological advancements.

The Future of Website Design: Trends to Watch

Website design is constantly changing, and businesses that stay ahead of trends create stronger user experiences and improve engagement. Here are some emerging trends shaping the future of website design:

1. AI-Powered Web Design

Artificial intelligence is making website creation easier and more personalized. Wix's **AI Website Builder** and **Wix ADI (Artificial Design Intelligence)** are already allowing users to generate custom websites in minutes. Moving forward, AI will help:

- Automate design elements based on user behavior.

- Improve chatbots for customer support.

- Generate dynamic content based on audience interests.

2. Voice Search Optimization

More people are using voice assistants like Siri, Alexa, and Google Assistant to browse the internet. Websites need to be optimized for voice searches by:

- Writing content in a conversational tone.

- Using long-tail keywords that match spoken queries.

- Structuring data properly for search engines to interpret easily.

3. Minimalist & Fast-Loading Websites

Web users expect fast load times and intuitive navigation. Some key trends include:

- Fewer animations and distractions for a cleaner look.

- Use of simple fonts and high-contrast color schemes.

- Optimized images and compressed files to improve speed.

4. Dark Mode & High-Contrast Design

Dark mode is becoming increasingly popular, reducing eye strain and improving readability. Many websites now offer a toggle between light and dark themes.

5. Mobile-First Design

With mobile browsing surpassing desktop use, websites need to prioritize mobile responsiveness. Future-proofing your site means:

- Ensuring it looks great on all screen sizes.

- Implementing mobile-friendly navigation and buttons.

- Using accelerated mobile pages (AMP) to boost speed.

6. Augmented Reality (AR) & Interactive Experiences

As AR technology improves, businesses will start integrating interactive experiences. This is especially useful for:

- **E-commerce** – Allowing customers to visualize products before buying.

- **Real Estate** – Offering virtual property tours.

- **Education** – Creating interactive learning environments.

7. Stronger Cybersecurity Measures

With increasing concerns over data privacy, website security is becoming a top priority. Wix already provides SSL certificates and secure hosting, but businesses should also:

- Use two-factor authentication for login security.

- Regularly update passwords and access permissions.

- Ensure GDPR compliance if collecting user data.

By keeping up with these trends, you can ensure your Wix website remains modern, user-friendly, and competitive in an ever-changing digital landscape.

This bonus chapter has provided valuable expert insights and free resources to help you maximize your Wix website's potential. By leveraging free tools, staying ahead of updates, and adapting to future design trends, you can create a high-performing site that continues to grow over time.

Stay proactive, keep learning, and embrace new technologies to ensure your website remains a powerful tool for your business or personal brand!

Final Thoughts & Next Steps
Summary of Key Takeaways

Building a successful website with Wix requires a combination of thoughtful design, strategic content, and continuous improvements. Throughout this guide, we have explored the essential aspects of creating and optimizing your site, from choosing the right template to implementing effective SEO strategies and troubleshooting common issues. Let's revisit some of the most critical lessons:

1. **Design with Purpose** – Your website's appearance should align with your brand identity and provide a seamless user experience. A clutter-free layout, high-quality images, and intuitive navigation are key factors.

2. **SEO is Essential** – To attract organic traffic, it's important to optimize your content with relevant keywords, proper metadata, and internal linking. Wix's built-in SEO tools, such as the Wix SEO Wiz, make this process easier.

3. **Mobile Responsiveness Matters** – A significant portion of website traffic comes from mobile users. Ensuring that your site is mobile-

Mega Jammy

friendly prevents usability issues and improves rankings on search engines.

4. **Loading Speed Impacts User Experience** – Slow-loading sites deter visitors. Optimize images, limit excessive animations, and use Wix's built-in performance tools to ensure fast load times.

5. **E-commerce Optimization Increases Sales** – For Wix store owners, a well-structured product page, clear CTAs, and a smooth checkout process are crucial for boosting conversions.

6. **Regular Updates Keep Your Site Relevant** – Outdated content or broken links can harm credibility. Periodic maintenance ensures that your website remains useful, secure, and engaging.

7. **Utilize Wix's Advanced Features** – Wix offers AI-driven tools, integrations, and marketing resources that enhance your site's functionality. Learning how to use these

features effectively can set your website apart from competitors.

Mastering these fundamental areas ensures that your Wix website operates at its full potential, whether it's a personal blog, an online store, or a professional portfolio.

Where to Go from Here: Learning More and Scaling Your Website

Now that you have built a strong foundation, the next step is continuous improvement and scaling. A website is not a static entity; it should evolve based on trends, user feedback, and business growth. Below are key strategies to take your website to the next level:

1. Keep Learning and Experimenting

Wix regularly updates its platform with new features, tools, and design capabilities. Staying informed about these updates allows you to take advantage of the latest enhancements. Consider:

- Following Wix's official blog and forums.

- Taking online courses on website development and digital marketing.

- Testing new layouts and features to optimize user experience.

2. Leverage Advanced SEO Strategies

If your goal is to drive more organic traffic, go beyond the basics:

- Implement structured data markup to help search engines understand your content.

- Create pillar content and topic clusters for stronger internal linking.

- Optimize for voice search by including conversational keywords.

- Conduct periodic SEO audits to refine your strategy.

3. Expand Your Marketing Efforts

Growth depends on visibility. To attract more visitors and potential customers, consider:

- Using **Wix Email Marketing** to send newsletters and promotions.

- Running targeted ad campaigns on Google and social media.

126

- Implementing a content marketing strategy with blog posts and videos.

- Partnering with influencers or affiliates to reach a wider audience.

4. Monetize Your Website

If you're looking to generate revenue, explore different monetization strategies:

- Sell digital products or services directly on your site.

- Offer online courses or memberships using Wix's subscription features.

- Monetize traffic through Google AdSense or sponsored content.

- Launch an affiliate marketing program where you earn commissions for referrals.

5. Enhance User Engagement and Retention

A loyal audience is key to long-term success. To keep visitors engaged:

- Enable Wix's chat feature for real-time customer support.

- Use pop-ups and lead magnets to encourage email sign-ups.

- Implement community-building tools, such as forums or interactive quizzes.

- Gather user feedback through surveys and analytics to refine your offerings.

6. Optimize for International Reach

If you want to expand beyond local audiences:

- Add multilingual support using Wix's translation tools.

- Implement currency converters and international payment options.

- Research global SEO strategies to attract visitors from different regions.

7. Integrate Automation for Efficiency

Time management becomes crucial as your website scales. Wix offers automation tools that can help streamline tasks:

- Automate social media posting with Wix's integrations.

128

- Set up email auto-responders for inquiries and sales confirmations.

- Use AI-powered chatbots to handle common customer questions.

- Schedule and manage bookings automatically for service-based businesses.

8. Invest in Professional Growth

To stay ahead of competitors, continuous skill development is key. Consider:

- Joining networking groups for entrepreneurs and web designers.

- Attending industry webinars and conferences.

- Hiring professionals for tasks like branding, copywriting, or advanced marketing.

- Collaborating with experts in SEO, content strategy, or paid advertising.

Final Words: Your Website's Journey is Just Beginning

Launching a website is a milestone, but maintaining and growing it is an ongoing process. By applying the insights shared in this book, you have the knowledge and tools to make your Wix website a lasting success.

Every successful website evolves based on user needs, technological advancements, and business goals. Whether your site is a passion project, an e-commerce store, or a service-based business, the key is to remain adaptable, curious, and willing to improve.

Here's to your success—may your Wix website not only meet but exceed your expectations!

About the Author

I am Mega Jammy, a seasoned digital entrepreneur, web designer, and online business consultant passionate about making website creation accessible to everyone. With years of experience helping businesses and individuals establish their online presence, I simplify complex web design concepts into easy-to-follow strategies. When not designing websites, I enjoy exploring emerging digital trends and teaching others how to harness technology for success.

131

www.ingramcontent.com/pod-product-compliance
Lightning Source LLC
LaVergne TN
LVHW022323060326
832902LV00020B/3637